Introduction

Welcome to the digital age, where opportunities to earn money online abound for those with the right mindset, skills, and determination.

In this book, we will embark on a journey through the vast landscape of online income streams, exploring various possibilities that can help you not only supplement your existing income but potentially create a sustainable and fulfilling online career.

Chapter 1:

The Foundation - Building Your Online Presence

In the vast and competitive landscape of the internet, establishing a strong foundation is key to your success in making money online. This chapter will guide you through the essential steps to build a solid online presence, ensuring that you stand out in the digital crowd.

Define Your Brand

Before you start exploring income streams, take the time to define your personal brand. Consider your skills, interests, and passions. What sets you apart from others? Understanding your unique value proposition will help you create a brand that resonates with your target audience.

Build a Professional Website

Your website is your virtual storefront. Whether you're freelancing, selling products, or offering services, having a professional and user-friendly site is crucial. Learn how to choose a domain name, design an appealing site, and optimize your site for search engines to increase visibility.

Leverage Social Media

Leverage, social media is a powerful tool for building connections and your brand. Explore different platforms and choose the ones for your goals. Learn how to create engaging content, build a social media to drive traffic to your website.

Networking in the Virtual World

Networking is as important online as it is offline. Join relevant online communities, forums, and social media groups to connect with like-minded individuals. Learn the art of networking, building genuine relationships, and leveraging your connections for opportunities.

Online Security and Privacy

As you establish your online presence, it's crucial to prioritize security and privacy. Learn about the importance of secure passwords, two-factor authentication, and encryption. Understand the potential risks of sharing personal information online and take steps to protect yourself.

Continuous Learning and Adaptability

The digital landscape is dynamic, with trends and technologies evolving rapidly. Embrace a mindset of continuous learning and adaptability. Stay updated on industry trends, technological advancements, and changes in online platforms to ensure your strategies remain effective.

Building Trust and Credibility

Trust is the currency of the digital world. Learn strategies for building trust and credibility with your audience. This includes providing valuable content, delivering on promises, and engaging authentically with your audience.

Analytics and Data Insights

Utilize analytics tools to gain insights into the performance of your online presence. Understand user behavior, track website traffic, and analyze social media metrics. Use this data to refine your strategies, identify areas for improvement, and capitalize on what works.

By the end of this chapter, you'll have laid a strong foundation for your online journey. Your brand will be well-defined, your online presence established, and you'll be ready to explore the diverse opportunities to earn money online in the subsequent chapters. Remember, building a successful online career is a journey, and the first step is a well-crafted and compelling online presence.

Chapter 2:

Freelancing - Your Skills, Your Income

Now that you've laid a solid foundation for your online presence, it's time to explore one of the most accessible and versatile ways to make money online: freelancing. Freelancing allows you to leverage your skills and expertise to work on projects for clients around the world. This chapter will guide you through the ins and outs of freelancing, helping you build a successful freelance career.

Identifying Your Skills

Start by identifying your skills and areas of expertise. Whether you're a writer, designer, programmer, marketer, or possess any other skill, there's likely a demand for your services. Consider your professional background, hobbies, and the skills you've developed over time.

Choosing the Right Freelance Platform

Freelance platforms serve as the bridge between freelancers and clients. Explore popular platforms such as Upwork, Fiverr, and Freelancer, and understand their features, fee structures, and user reviews. Choose a platform that aligns with your skills and offers a supportive environment for freelancers.

Crafting an Outstanding Profile

Your profile on a freelance platform is your virtual resume. Learn how to create a compelling profile that showcases your skills, experience, and personality. Include a professional photo, write a captivating bio, and highlight your achievements to stand out from the competition.

Setting Your Rates

Determining your freelance rates can be challenging but is crucial for both you and your clients. Understand how to set competitive yet fair rates based on factors such as your skills, experience, and the complexity of the tasks. Be transparent about your pricing to build trust with potential clients.

Writing Winning Proposals

To secure freelance projects, you need to submit compelling proposals. Learn the art of crafting personalized and persuasive proposals that address the client's needs. Highlight your relevant experience, propose a clear solution, and showcase your enthusiasm for the project.

Delivering High-Quality Work

Consistently delivering high-quality work is essential for building a positive reputation as a freelancer. Understand client expectations, communicate effectively, and meet deadlines. Satisfied clients are more likely to provide positive reviews and become repeat customers.

Building a Freelance Portfolio

As you complete projects, build a freelance portfolio to showcase your best work. Include case studies, testimonials, and before-and-after examples if applicable. A well-curated portfolio serves as a powerful marketing tool when attracting new clients.

Scaling Your Freelance Business

Once you've established yourself as a freelancer, explore ways to scale your business. Consider raising your rates, expanding your service offerings, and building long-term relationships with clients. Explore opportunities to collaborate with other freelancers or even create an agency.

Freelancing provides a flexible and accessible way to earn money online. Whether you're looking for a side hustle or aiming for a full-time freelance career, mastering the art of freelancing will open doors to a world of opportunities. In the next chapters, we'll explore additional avenues for online income, each with its unique set of challenges and rewards.

Chapter 3:

Blogging and Content Creation - Sharing Your Passion

Blogging and content creation offer an avenue to turn your passion or expertise into a source of income. In this chapter, we'll explore the world of creating content online, from starting a blog to monetizing your creative efforts.

Choosing Your Niche

Selecting a niche is a crucial first step in the world of blogging. Identify topics that align with your interests, knowledge, and the interests of your target audience. A well-defined niche helps you stand out and attract a dedicated readership.

Setting Up Your Blog

Now that you have a niche, it's time to set up your blog. Explore popular blogging platforms like WordPress, Blogger, or Medium. Learn the basics of designing an attractive and user-friendly blog, and optimize it for search engines to enhance discoverability.

Creating Compelling Content

Content is king in the blogging world. Learn how to create engaging, informative, and shareable content. Explore different types of content, including blog posts, infographics, videos, and podcasts. Consistency is key, so establish a content calendar to maintain a regular posting schedule.

Building Your Audience

Growing a loyal audience is essential for the success of your blog. Utilize social media, email marketing, and other promotional strategies to drive traffic to your blog. Engage with your audience through comments and social media, fostering a sense of community around your content.

Monetizing Your Blog

Once you've built a solid readership, explore various monetization strategies. This can include advertising, sponsored content, affiliate marketing, and selling digital or physical products. Diversifying your income streams can provide stability and sustainability.

Affiliate Marketing for Bloggers

Dive deeper into the world of affiliate marketing specifically tailored for bloggers. Learn how to incorporate affiliate links seamlessly into your content, choose relevant products or services to promote, and optimize your strategy for maximizing commissions.

Sponsored Content and Partnerships

As your blog gains popularity, brands may approach you for sponsored content or partnerships. Understand how to negotiate fair deals, maintain authenticity in sponsored content, and choose partnerships that align with your brand and audience.

Scaling Your Content Business

Explore ways to scale your content creation business. This may involve hiring additional writers, expanding your content formats, or even creating a network of blogs. Scaling requires strategic planning to maintain quality while increasing your output.

By the end of this chapter, you'll have a solid understanding of the blogging and content creation landscape. Whether you're a hobbyist looking to share your passion or an aspiring content creator aiming for a full-time career, blogging provides a platform for self-expression and financial opportunity. In the following chapters, we'll continue our exploration of diverse online income streams, each offering its unique set of possibilities.

Chapter 4:

E-commerce - Turning Ideas into Profit

E-commerce is a dynamic and ever-expanding realm that allows you to transform your ideas into profitable ventures. In this chapter, we'll delve into the world of online selling, covering everything from choosing products to marketing and scaling your e-commerce business.

Identifying Profitable Products

The first step in building an e-commerce business is identifying products that have market demand. Explore trends, conduct market research, and assess your interests to find a niche that aligns with both your passion and profit potential. Consider whether you'll sell physical products, digital goods, or a combination of both.

Choosing the Right E-commerce Platform

Selecting the right e-commerce platform is crucial for your business's success. Platforms like Shopify, WooCommerce, and BigCommerce offer various features and scalability options. Understand the pros and cons of each platform, and choose the one that best suits your business model and technical requirements.

Building a User-Friendly Online Store

Your online store is the face of your business. Learn how to design an attractive and user-friendly website that encourages visitors to make purchases. Optimize product pages, implement secure payment gateways, and ensure a smooth checkout process to enhance the overall shopping experience.

Implementing Dropshipping

Consider the dropshipping model as a low-risk way to start your e-commerce journey. With dropshipping, you sell products without handling inventory or fulfillment. Learn how to find reliable suppliers, optimize product listings, and manage customer expectations in a dropshipping business.

Marketing Your E-commerce Business

Effective marketing is essential for driving traffic and sales to your online store. Explore various digital marketing strategies, including social media marketing, search engine optimization (SEO), email marketing, and paid advertising. Develop a comprehensive marketing plan to reach your target audience.

Customer Service and Satisfaction

Exceptional customer service is a cornerstone of a successful e-commerce business. Implement efficient communication channels, address customer inquiries promptly, and resolve issues with professionalism. Positive reviews and satisfied customers contribute significantly to the growth of your business.

Scaling Your E-commerce Business

As your business gains traction, explore strategies for scaling your e-commerce operations. This may involve expanding your product range, optimizing your supply chain, and exploring international markets. Consider automating repetitive tasks to streamline operations and accommodate increased demand.

Exploring Print on Demand and Custom Products

Diversify your product offerings by exploring print-on-demand services and custom products. This allows you to offer unique and personalized items without the need for large upfront investments. Learn how to collaborate with print-on-demand providers and integrate these products into your store.

By the end of this chapter, you'll have a comprehensive understanding of how to start and scale your e-commerce business. Whether you're selling handmade crafts, dropshipping popular products, or creating custom merchandise, e-commerce opens doors to a wide range of possibilities. In the following chapters, we'll continue our exploration of diverse online income streams, each presenting unique opportunities for financial success.

Chapter 5:

Online Courses and Consulting - Sharing Your Expertise

If you have specialized knowledge or skills in a particular field, monetizing your expertise through online courses and consulting can be a rewarding venture. In this chapter, we'll explore how to create and market online courses, offer consulting services, and build a thriving career as an expert in your niche.

Identifying Your Expertise

Start by identifying your expertise or skills that have market demand. This could be anything from digital marketing and programming to fitness training or life coaching. Reflect on your professional background and passions to pinpoint areas where you can provide valuable insights.

Creating and Selling Online Courses

Online courses are a popular way to share knowledge and generate income. Learn how to structure and create compelling courses that cater to your target audience. Explore platforms like Udemy, Teachable, or Skillshare to host and sell your courses. Consider creating a dedicated website to showcase your expertise and courses.

Setting Up Consulting Services

Consulting allows you to offer personalized advice and guidance to individuals or businesses. Determine the specific areas in which you can provide consulting services. This could involve strategy consulting, business coaching, career counseling, or any other specialized field.

Building Credibility as an Expert

Establishing yourself as an expert is crucial for attracting clients to your courses or consulting services. Develop a strong online presence through blogging, social media, and participation in relevant forums. Share valuable insights, case studies, and success stories to build credibility in your field.

Marketing Your Courses and Services

Effective marketing is key to reaching a broader audience. Develop a marketing strategy that includes social media promotion, email campaigns, and collaborations with influencers or industry leaders. Utilize your online presence to showcase your expertise and attract potential clients.

Providing Exceptional Value

Whether through courses or consulting, providing exceptional value is essential for building a positive reputation. Tailor your offerings to meet the needs of your clients or students. Collect and showcase testimonials to demonstrate the impact of your expertise on others.

Creating Webinars and Workshops

Expand your reach by offering webinars and workshops. These live sessions allow you to interact directly with your audience, answer questions, and provide real-time value. Webinars can serve as both a marketing tool and an additional revenue stream.

Scaling Your Online Expertise Business

Explore ways to scale your online expertise business. This may involve creating additional courses, expanding your consulting services, or building a team to assist with course creation and client management. Consider leveraging automation tools to streamline administrative tasks.

By the end of this chapter, you'll have a roadmap for turning your expertise into a lucrative online career. Whether you choose to focus on online courses, consulting, or a combination of both, sharing your knowledge with a global audience offers the potential for significant financial success. In the following chapters, we'll continue our exploration of diverse online income streams, each presenting unique opportunities for financial growth.

Chapter 6:

Stock Photography and Creative Assets - Turning Creativity into Cash

For those with a passion for photography, graphic design, or other artistic endeavors, the world of stock photography and creative assets provides an exciting avenue to monetize your creativity. In this chapter, we'll explore how you can turn your artistic talents into a source of income by creating and selling stock photos, illustrations, videos, and other digital assets.

Creating Marketable Content

Start by creating high-quality and marketable content. This could include stunning photographs, eye-catching illustrations, compelling videos, or even audio clips. Pay attention to trends in the stock asset marketplace and tailor your creations to meet the demands of potential buyers.

Choosing the Right Stock Platforms

Numerous stock platforms exist where you can showcase and sell your creative assets. Explore popular platforms such as Shutterstock, Adobe Stock, iStock, and others. Understand the submission guidelines, licensing options, and payment structures of each platform before getting started.

Understanding Licensing and Rights

Before uploading your content, familiarize yourself with licensing terms and rights. Different stock platforms offer various licensing options, including royalty-free and rights-managed. Determine the licensing model that aligns with your goals and ensures fair compensation for your work.

Building a Diverse Portfolio

Diversify your portfolio to appeal to a broader audience. Include a variety of subjects, styles, and formats in your collection. This not only increases your chances of making sales but also showcases your versatility as a creative contributor.

Marketing Your Creative Assets

While stock platforms handle the transactions, marketing your creative assets is essential to attract buyers. Leverage social media, personal websites, and online communities to promote your portfolio. Use captivating visuals and keyword optimization to enhance the discoverability of your work.

Collaborating with Brands and Agencies

Explore opportunities to collaborate with brands and creative agencies. They may seek custom photography or design work for specific projects. Building relationships with clients in addition to selling stock assets can lead to recurring business and additional income.

Staying Informed About Trends

Stay informed about current design and photography trends. This allows you to create content that aligns with market demands and increases the likelihood of your work being featured prominently on stock platforms. Regularly update your portfolio to stay relevant.

Scaling Your Creative Business

As you gain experience and recognition in the stock photography and creative asset space, consider scaling your business. This may involve expanding your portfolio, collaborating with other creatives, or even launching your own brand. Explore opportunities to license your work for broader commercial use.

By the end of this chapter, you'll have a solid understanding of how to transform your creativity into a lucrative venture through stock photography and creative assets. Whether you're a photographer, illustrator, or graphic designer, this online income stream offers the potential for financial success while allowing you to showcase and monetize your artistic talents. In the following chapters, we'll continue our exploration of diverse online income streams, each presenting unique opportunities for financial growth.

Chapter 7:

Affiliate Marketing - Partnerships for Profit

Affiliate marketing is a powerful online income stream that allows you to earn commissions by promoting other people's products or services. In this chapter, we'll delve into the world of affiliate marketing, exploring how to choose the right programs, effectively promote products, and build a sustainable income through strategic partnerships.

Understanding Affiliate Marketing Basics

Begin by understanding the fundamentals of affiliate marketing. Grasp the concept of affiliate programs, where merchants pay you a commission for driving traffic or sales to their websites through your unique affiliate links. Familiarize yourself with the various payment models, including pay-per-sale, pay-per-click, and pay-per-lead.

Choosing Profitable Affiliate Programs

Selecting the right affiliate programs is crucial for success. Consider products or services that align with your niche and are likely to resonate with your audience. Research the reputation of the affiliate programs, their commission rates, and the quality of the products or services they offer.

Integrating Affiliate Links Naturally

Effective affiliate marketing involves seamlessly integrating affiliate links into your content. Learn how to incorporate these links naturally within blog posts, articles, videos, or social media content. Avoid being overly promotional; instead, focus on providing value and genuine recommendations.

Creating Compelling Content

Content is key to successful affiliate marketing. Craft compelling and informative content that addresses the needs and interests of your audience. Whether through reviews, tutorials, or recommendations, your content should build trust and encourage your audience to take action.

Building an Email List for Affiliate Marketing

Building an email list is a powerful strategy for affiliate marketing. Capture the email addresses of your audience and nurture the relationship through regular communication. Utilize email marketing to share valuable content, exclusive promotions, and affiliate offers.

Analyzing Affiliate Performance

Regularly analyze the performance of your affiliate marketing efforts. Track clicks, conversions, and commissions to understand which products and strategies are most effective. Use analytics tools provided by affiliate programs or third-party platforms to gain insights into your audience's behavior.

Ethical Affiliate Marketing Practices

Maintain ethical practices in your affiliate marketing endeavors. Disclose your affiliate relationships transparently to your audience. Only promote products or services that you genuinely believe in, and avoid misleading or deceptive marketing tactics. Trust and credibility are paramount in affiliate marketing.

Scaling Your Affiliate Marketing Business

As you gain experience and your audience grows, explore ways to scale your affiliate marketing business. This may involve diversifying the products you promote, expanding into new niches, or collaborating with other affiliates. Consider negotiating higher commission rates as your influence increases.

By the end of this chapter, you'll have a comprehensive understanding of how to harness the power of affiliate marketing to generate income online. Whether you're a blogger, content creator, or social media influencer, affiliate marketing offers a versatile and scalable way to monetize your online presence. In the following chapters, we'll continue our exploration of diverse online income streams, each presenting unique opportunities for financial growth.

Chapter 8:

Cryptocurrency and Online Investments - Navigating the Digital Financial Landscape

The world of cryptocurrency and online investments presents a unique opportunity to grow your wealth in the digital age. In this chapter, we'll explore the basics of cryptocurrency, online investment platforms, and strategies to make informed financial decisions in the ever-evolving digital financial landscape.

Understanding Cryptocurrency

Begin by gaining a fundamental understanding of cryptocurrency. Explore the concept of blockchain technology, decentralized finance (DeFi), and the various cryptocurrencies available, such as Bitcoin, Ethereum, and altcoins. Recognize the potential benefits and risks associated with investing in this dynamic market.

Choosing a Cryptocurrency Exchange

To participate in the cryptocurrency market, you'll need to choose a reliable cryptocurrency exchange. Research and compare different platforms based on factors like security, fees, available cryptocurrencies, and user experience. Popular exchanges include Coinbase, Binance, and Kraken.

Building a Diversified Crypto Portfolio

Diversification is key to managing risk in cryptocurrency investments. Learn how to build a diversified portfolio by investing in different cryptocurrencies with varying use cases and risk profiles. Consider factors like market capitalization, project fundamentals, and long-term potential.

Staying Informed About Market Trends

Stay informed about market trends and developments in the cryptocurrency space. Regularly follow reputable news sources, subscribe to industry newsletters, and participate in online communities to stay updated. Awareness of market trends is crucial for making informed investment decisions.

Exploring Online Investment Platforms

Beyond cryptocurrency, explore other online investment platforms that align with your financial goals. Consider robo-advisors, peer-to-peer lending platforms, and real estate crowdfunding. Each platform comes with its own set of risks and potential returns, so conduct thorough research before investing.

Setting Financial Goals and Risk Tolerance

Define your financial goals and assess your risk tolerance before making investment decisions. Determine whether you're investing for short-term gains, long-term growth, or a specific financial milestone. Understanding your risk tolerance helps you make strategic investment choices aligned with your objectives.

Implementing Dollar-Cost Averaging

Dollar-cost averaging is a strategy where you consistently invest a fixed amount of money at regular intervals, regardless of the asset's price. Learn how this strategy helps mitigate the impact of market volatility and potentially enhance long-term returns.

Practicing Secure Online Investing

Prioritize security when engaging in online investing. Implement strong passwords, enable two-factor authentication, and use secure and reputable platforms. Be cautious of phishing scams and fraudulent investment schemes, and only invest through well-established and regulated platforms.

By the end of this chapter, you'll have a foundational understanding of how to navigate the digital financial landscape through cryptocurrency and online investments. Whether you're exploring the potential of decentralized finance or seeking diversified investment opportunities, the digital world offers a range of options to grow your wealth. In the following chapters, we'll continue our exploration of diverse online income streams, each presenting unique opportunities for financial growth.

Impressum :
Maik Fürste
aercorpus@gmx.net